ADMISSION OF KANSAS.

SPEECH

OF

HON. MARCUS J. PARROTT,

OF KANSAS.

Delivered in the House of Representatives, April 10, 1860.

WASHINGTON, D. C.
BUELL & BLANCHARD, PRINTERS.
1860.

Speech of Mr. Parrott.

The House having under consideration the bill (H. R. No. 23) for the admission of Kansas into the Union—

Mr. PARROTT said:

Mr. SPEAKER: I do not propose, under all the circumstances, to inflict on the House an elaborate speech in regard to the merely political questions connected with Kansas Territory; but I should do injustice, both to myself and to my constituents, if I did not come forward and meet the objections brought by the gentleman who has made the minority report. I shall do so in a spirit of frankness and candor, submitting myself fairly, and cheerfully even, to interrogatories from all sides of the House. I will say more: if any reasonable man shall believe that I have not fairly met every objection that has been made, I will give up this controversy, go out of the House, and ask my constituents to send somebody here who does understand their case. The cause itself is unanswerable. I shall meet, then, every objection, and meet it fairly and squarely.

When the Lecompton Constitution was adjudged to be a fraud, two years ago, in this House, and when, with a singular stultification, as it seems to me, men could be found in this House ready to pronounce it a fraud, and at the same time to tender it to the people of Kansas as their organic law; when, I say, that Constitution was stricken down, there sprung out of it that mean and false contrivance known as the English bill.

The title of that bill was a false title; its provisions were deceitful and double. It is entitled "An act to admit the State of Kansas into the Union," when everybody knows that it was intended to keep the State of Kansas out of the Union. For, sir, we all know that the people of the Territory had rejected the Lecompton Constitution. They sent a Delegate to this House to protest against its acceptance, which protest I entered early and often during that controversy. It was known they had rejected it, when, on a specific issue made, they polled a vote of five thousand majority against it, in January of 1858; and it was, moreover, known that that Lecompton Constitution, which was pretended to be ratified in December of 1857, was the culminating point of a long series of frauds and aggressions on the rights of the people of the Territory.

Sir, I was amazed, the other day, to hear the distinguished member from Alabama, [Mr. CURRY,] who has a reputation for ingenuousness, paying posthumous honors to the Lecompton Constitution. I ask that gentleman to look at the votes polled in certain precincts in the December election of 1857, in the pretended submission of the Lecompton Constitution. Let him look at Oxford, and Kickapoo, and Delaware Crossing, and compare the vote then reported with the returns from those precincts at every general election since, up to this time, and note the disparity. The mustered clans and hosts of December, 1857, at Oxford and Kickapoo, whither have they gone? Ask the political conjurers who summoned these mythical myriads to appear upon the stage for the accomplishment of sinister designs.

At no election since that pretended affair, have all these precincts combined polled more than three or four hundred votes; and yet, sir, if you subtract the thousands which were polled there in December, 1857, you would have the Lecompton Constitution left naked—stripped of the factitious vote through which it was sought to be juggled off upon the credulity of Congress and the country.

Sir, I do not know that I should myself be politically displeased to find that those who differ with me honestly and conscientiously, regarding the policy of our country in respect to slavery, are so far pressed to the wall as to stand and plant themselves upon the ground of the Lecompton Constitution. It is, sir, a confession of weakness; and I am not at all apprehensive that the judgment of history will be disturbed or misled in regard to the merits of that measure. That judgment has been already pronounced in every section of the country; for, has not a distinguished Senator [Mr. HAMMOND] of South Carolina said, in language, if not very elegant, at least idiomatic, that it ought to have been "kicked out of Congress" the moment it was presented there?

But, sir, this English bill was a proposition odious and offensive to the people of the Territory. It was hardly less revolting, I hope, to the country at large, on account of its intense discrimination against the institutions of the free States. It prescribes one rule for the admission of a slave State, and another, with superadded and onerous conditions, for a free State. It is thus partial, invidious, and unfair. What have the people of Kansas said in reply? In effect, "We desire admission into the Union, 'but not such admission; we desire, if we 'come into the Union, to come with our honor 'untarnished and unsullied—on an equal footing with the original States—not only as a 'confederate, but as a coequal in the family of 'States."

I shall say nowhere, in the course of my remarks, that the people of Kansas have succumbed to the provisions of the English bill. I should despise myself and dishonor them if I believed they ever had it in contemplation to give way to its provisions. What next, sir? They have seen fit to form another Constitution, and the President of the United States has come forward, and, in language nearly identical with that of the minority report, addressed to the Thirty-fifth Congress, has anticipated the formation of the Constitution, and declared it to be a revolutionary act.

Mr. BARKSDALE. I understood the gentleman to say just now that the people of Kansas have not succumbed to the English bill.

Mr. PARROTT. Yes, sir.

Mr. BARKSDALE. I desire to ask him if they did not vote under its provisions?

Mr. PARROTT. I will answer that they did vote, but they were not parties to that law. They repudiated its restrictive clause as inoperative, for reasons which I shall presently state. I ask you—I put it to the gentleman from Mississippi—whether it could be fairly said that, having rejected the Lecompton Constitution, they were bound by all the provisions of that bill?

Mr. BARKSDALE. Why, sir, I hold that they were bound by the provisions of that bill. That is the point which I have made. Whether they voted or not, it was their duty to do it; and I hold it was their duty to obey all the provisions of that bill. Hence I am opposed to the admission of Kansas upon that very ground: that she would be admitted in palpable violation of the law passed by Congress.

Mr. PARROTT. I must pass on, Mr. Speaker. The people of Kansas have presented another Constitution here, and I wish, before I advance to the consideration of specific objections——

Mr. COX. Before the gentleman leaves that point, I beg that he will allow me to ask him a question.

Mr. PARROTT. I yield to the gentleman for that purpose.

Mr. COX. He says that the people of Kansas never, in any way, recognised that bill of the conference committee. Is that his statement?

Mr. PARROTT. I said they had never succumbed to the *restrictive* provisions of that bill.

Mr. COX. Oh, no; you did not use the words "restrictive provisions."

Mr. PARROTT. Well, I say that now, and I said that before.

Mr. COX. Well, I ask my friend, in justice to the men who voted for that bill, to answer this question——

Mr. PARROTT. I do not want to be drawn from the line of my argument.

Mr. COX. Ah, but the gentleman must state the truth as it occurred there, and it is this: that, in pursuance of the provisions of that bill, clearly followed in every particular by the commissioners, there was an election in Kansas; and by that election, the sense of the people was taken, and Lecompton, as the chairman of the Committee on Territories said this morning, was throttled and killed by it; and it was intended, by many of the men who voted for that bill, to give that very opportunity to the people to break down that Constitution which they spurned.

Mr. PARROTT. The gentleman is vindicating his own action, and not asking me a question. I cannot yield for such a purpose.

Mr. COX. The gentleman knows that Governor Denver himself, by official proclamation, following up the provisions of that conference bill, proclaimed the number of votes cast, and at the end of his proclamation, in pursuance of that very conference bill, declared that the Lecompton Constitution was not the choice of the people of Kansas.

Mr. PARROTT. I cannot yield any longer to the gentleman. He does not interrogate me.

Mr. MONTGOMERY. Will the gentleman

from Kansas allow me to answer the gentleman from Ohio?

Mr. PARROTT. No; I must decline to yield further. I shall come to that point presently.

Mr. MONTGOMERY. I will do it in one minute.

Mr. PARROTT. I am coming to that directly. I was about to say, when I was interrupted, that this case is to be discriminated from preceding applications made by this Territory for admission into the Union. Kansas has once been admitted by the House of Representatives as a State; upon another occasion, it has been admitted by the Senate; and upon a third occasion, when both houses conjoined to invite her into the Union, the proposals were declined. But, sir, these were contests of factions; they rested upon peculiar and political grounds, and not upon arguments of the intrinsic fitness of the Territory to become a State, by reason of the numbers, the homogenousness, the aggregate or distributive wealth of its people, or any argument of economy. It is due to candor that thus much should be stated.

These preceding applications were urged on the ground of political necessity, arising out of the confusion and disorder prevalent in the Territory. For example: the Topeka Constitution was passed by those friendly to the establishment of free institutions, because the Territorial Government had been wrested from the hands of the settlers, and there was no legal relief, except in the adoption of that Constitution. The Lecompton Constitution was passed for exactly opposite reasons, because the usurpers and invaders would be driven out of the Territory, and all their years of struggle, and the unripe fruits of invasion, would be thrown away, unless that Constitution could be ratified by Congress. But this is a different case; it stands upon the intrinsic fitness of the country to become a State. The Territorial Legislature initiated the measure by passing a law for the regulation of the subject. Admonished by the haste and imperfection of previous attempts in this behalf, they now prepared to move forward by slow and gradual steps, consulting the people at every stage, so that if, at any time, from first to last, the popular voice failed to buoy up the movement, it must drop and be lost—the whole scheme failed. In the first place, the specific question was submitted, whether the change was desirable; and it was passed upon as a separate and distinct question, unmixed with anything else, at an election appointed for that purpose only. It occasioned but little surprise to me that this question failed to elicit a vote proportioned to its great importance, and a much less universal expression than could be desired in a business of this magnitude.

In the first place, abstract questions of this kind rarely engage, ardently and deeply, the popular attention; but in the present case, I attribute the light vote chiefly to the fact that the public mind, long kept on a tension straining after the public safety, naturally underwent a reaction, and inclined to repose when the sense of immediate danger no longer threatened. The summing up of the vote showed a majority of five to one in favor of the State movement. In the next place, the Convention having been called, came an election for delegates to represent the people therein. This question excited a universal interest and a warm contest in every district of the Territory. The delegates were chosen; the Convention met; a Constitution was framed. It was submitted for ratification some two months after its adoption by the Convention and its publication and circulation among the people. The election was again a special one, for this purpose, and for this alone. The Constitution was ratified by two-thirds of the votes cast; and I think I may reasonably assume, that but for false arguments employed to mislead the public mind in respect to some material clauses of the instrument — particularly the article on suffrage—the vote against it would have been wholly insignificant. In point of fact, therefore, the Constitution may be taken as acceptable to nearly the entire body of the people of the Territory. Nor does this approval stand alone. The sober second thought of the people is not wanting; for it was put in issue again in the election of a Delegate, among whose prominent duties would be that which I am now attempting to perform, to wit: the pressing of the Constitution upon Congress; and in this the former emphatic expression was renewed. Finally, a third time, this judgment was reaffirmed in electing State officers and a State Legislature from the ranks of the party friendly to the Constitution. Thus it appears now, beyond doubt or cavil, that the public interest and approval, not strong in the first part, rose at last to a height of zeal corresponding to the magnitude of the movement, and bore up by heavy and repeated verdicts, through many trials, the friends of a State Government under this Constitution.

This much is clear, and can form no part of any controversy arising out of the consideration of this subject: that the people of the Territory did, deliberately and dispassionately, demand a Convention to frame a Constitution and State Government; that they constituted a Convention of delegates, freely and fairly chosen from among themselves, to make such Constitution; and, finally, that they did thrice declare their entire and unqualified approval and acceptance of the instrument framed and submitted to them by the Convention. No part of this ground is debatable.

The first inquiry which presents itself is, were the people in the exercise of a legitimate power in doing what they have done? The practice of the Government has not been uniform in respect to the preliminary steps towards a State Government. In some instances, perhaps in most, Congress has authorized the people, by what is called an enabling act, to frame a Constitution preparatory to application for admission into the Union; in other, and not a few instances, the people have proceeded on their own motion, as in this case. I am not aware that their right to do so has ever been seriously called in question; at any rate, it is safe to say that the exercise of this power by the people has never been deprecated or condemned by Congress as illegal or revolutionary.

This right is now put in issue. It is said by the President of the United States, and said by the distinguished gentleman from Missouri, [Mr. CLARK,] whose signature is appended to this minority report, that the people of Kansas had no right to make a Constitution. Mr. Speaker, there are few political heresies known to the world that this Administration has not fallen into, and one of the worst and most injurious to our progressive society is the dogma in which he announces that one Congress cannot repeal a law made by another Congress; that our laws, like those of the Medes and Persians, are irreversible. I now pass to consider whether the people of a Territory can be restricted of a constitutional privilege, and whether this act is such a privilege.

Mr. CLARK, of Missouri. Will the gentleman from Kansas allow me to say——

Mr. PARROTT. I cannot yield now. I am at this moment speaking of the President. I will come to you in a moment. [Laughter.] The President says, in his message to the Thirty-fifth Congress, second session, he does not presume the people of Kansas will have the hardihood to frame another Constitution without the consent of Congress. And now, sir, what is the application of the people of Kansas upon which we are now to act, but an application upon their part to Congress to repeal the restrictive clause of the English bill? Is it lawless for the people of Kansas to petition Congress for a redress of their grievances? That, sir, is no new question; but it presents the very point in issue. In the year 1836, in the case of Arkansas, this whole question was presented, discussed, and decided—that the presentation of a Constitution, framed by a Constitutional Convention, was nothing but an exercise of the great constitutional prerogative of the people to petition Congress for a redress of their grievances. And this is the mode; this is the particular degree of relief for which they have prayed.

Attorney General Butler, speaking of this Arkansas case, said, in relation to the right of the people of a Territory in this respect:

"They undoubtedly possess the ordinary privileges and immunities of citizens of the United States. Among these is the right of the people peaceably to assemble and petition the Government for the redress of grievances. In the exercise of this right, the inhabitants * * * may meet together in primary assemblies or in Convention * * * for the purpose of petitioning Congress to abrogate the Territorial Government, and to admit them into the Union as an independent State. The particular form which they may give to their petition cannot be material, so long as they confine themselves to the mere right of petitioning, and conduct all their proceedings in a peaceable manner. If, therefore, they see proper to accompany their petition by a written Constitution, framed and agreed on by them, * * * I perceive no legal objection to their right to do so."

So I say now, to the gentleman from Missouri. When he assumes that the people of Kansas are guilty of lawlessness, because they have assembled in Convention, I tell him that his English bill is inoperative and void, because it is in contravention of the right guarantied by the Constitution to the people, peaceably to assemble and petition Congress for a redress of their grievances.

But, sir, right here let me observe to that gentleman, that there is another point to which I wish to call his attention. He has been very free in bringing in a bill of indictment against the people whom I represent; and I must be allowed to observe, with all due respect to him, that it comes with peculiar infelicity from a citizen of Missouri in his place here to charge the people of Kansas with lawlessness and disorder. All now see clearly the true aspect of this feature of the case, notwithstanding the most industrious efforts have been made to conceal it from the public eye. It is now known, as well as anything ever can or will be known, that it was the repeated raids of ruffians and cut-throats of Missouri, with a view to overwhelm the infant settlements of the Territory, that first set burning in Kansas Territory the fire that afterwards spread all over the land, and recently broke out with such fatal fierceness at Harper's Ferry, in Virginia.

Mr. CLARK, of Missouri. I ask the gentleman to allow me to say that he is in great error, both in his remarks and in the spirit in which he delivers them, against the people of Missouri.

Mr. PARROTT. I was not speaking of the people of Missouri.

Mr. CLARK, of Missouri. The gentleman was in error, as the history of the times will show.

Mr. PARROTT. The gentleman must not take up my time by going into a prolonged discussion of that matter; we can do that, if necessary, another time.

Mr. CLARK, of Missouri. I just want to say that the history of the times will show that it was, if men went into Kansas from Missouri for unlawful purposes, they were instigated to go there by the persons who were selected and sent out by the emigrant aid societies of New England. [Laughter on the Republican side.]

Mr. THAYER. The gentleman from Kansas yields to me to reply to the remark of the gentleman from Missouri [Mr. CLARK] in relation to the New England Emigrant Aid Company. On several occasions I have sought the floor, when charges have been made here against that company, for the purpose of showing what it was, and how it acted. I have, in one speech made in this hall, defined its operations; I have shown it to be simply a business organization, conducted on business principles, for the purpose of making investments in the Territory of Kansas. They never paid any one's expenses to that Territory; they never expended one dollar in the purchase of arms for any of the people who went to that Territory; they never made any contributions of money in the shape of gifts at any time; they had in view simply and always legitimate business purposes; and if they failed to conduct their operations upon legitimate business principles, they were amenable to the courts of justice whenever they violated the rules that govern business corporations; but that has never been charged; no suit has ever been brought against them.

Mr. REAGAN. Will the gentleman from Massachusetts permit me to ask him whether the project of this emigrant aid project did not originate amongst politicians in Washington city, for the accomplishment of political purposes?

Mr. THAYER. No, sir. On the contrary, I originated the plan myself. I framed the charter of that Emigrant Aid Company. I laid every timber in the plan of its organization, and am alone responsible for it. I was a member of the Massachusetts Legislature at the time; and if the Kansas and Nebraska bill had not passed, I would have applied the energies of the company to some other purpose; but that bill having passed, I thought it opened a very good field for operation.

Mr. REAGAN. Will the gentleman allow me to propound another question?

Mr. PARROTT. I must object to my time being consumed by this interlocutory discussion.

Mr. REAGAN. I only wished to ask the gentleman whether the plan had not previously been set on foot here, in Washington, by Senators and Representatives in Congress, to accomplish a political purpose?

The SPEAKER *pro tempore*. The Chair must arrest this irregular discussion, unless the gentleman from Kansas yields.

Mr. PARROTT. I cannot yield, unless the House will extend my time.

Mr. THAYER. If the gentleman from Kansas is willing to give me the opportunity, I should be glad to answer the gentleman from Texas; and I ask him to repeat his question.

Mr. REAGAN. What I asked was, whether the movement of which he speaks in Massachusetts, was not subsequent to the setting on foot of a scheme for an emigrant aid society in this city, by politicians, for political purposes, during the winter of 1854.

Mr. THAYER. On the contrary, that was subsequent to the origin of this Emigrant Aid Company in Massachusetts. As early as February, 1854, the plan of this company was formed and published in Massachusetts. The Kansas and Nebraska bill was not passed until May, in that year, and some movement was made by politicians here in Washington relative to some kind of a society to settle Kansas, I think in June or July of that year. But this Washington scheme never was put in operation. If there was anything that took precedence of this emigrant aid organization, it was the blue lodges of Missouri, [laughter,] which were, I believe, formed prior to that time; and which had resolved that the Yankees should never go into Kansas, if bayonets and revolvers could keep them out. The Emigrant Aid Society, however, never sent any men there except peaceable men, who went to Kansas for peaceable and friendly purposes. The company never so much as inquired what were their politics. Among its original corporators were Whigs, Democrats, and Free-Soilers. If its labors and investments and encouragement of emigration have resulted in making Kansas a free State, as gentlemen claim, I have only to say it was done according to law.

Mr. CLARK, of Missouri. Will the gentleman permit me to say——

Mr. PARROTT. I cannot yield further. I cannot stop now to discuss emigrant aid societies or blue lodges. I know all about those companies. I received no aid in going to Kansas myself, and I believe a vast majority of the people who went to Kansas went there without the aid of the New England Emigrant Aid Society, though the efforts of that association were doubtless well meant. I am discussing the charge brought forward against my constituency; and I wish to say, now and here, that it is false and slanderous to charge that they have ever resisted the laws of the United States, or that they are disloyal or revolutionary, either in any part of their history or in their present attitude.

Mr. CLARK, of Missouri. I ask the gentleman if history will prove that the people of Kansas have not resisted indictments?

Mr. PARROTT. I am going to tell you about that in a few moments.

Mr. SMITH, of Virginia. I object to these interruptions.

Mr. CLARK, of Missouri. And I wish to ask the gentleman, at the same time, whether he intended to apply the language, "false and slanderous," to me?

Mr. PARROTT. Not at all. I disclaim any disrespect to the gentleman from Missouri. I am answering the gentleman's argument. I am answering a printed argument addressed to this House; and, if the judgment of this House be that I am trespassing upon its rules of order,

I will not pursue this line of remark further. [Cries of "Go on!" "Go on!"]

Mr. Speaker, the gentleman from Missouri [Mr. CLARK] wants me to tell him whether the people of Kansas have not resisted indictments. God forbid that I should ever deny that the people of Kansas did resist the execution of the Territorial laws. That, sir, in my judgment, constitutes one of the chiefest glories of that people in their memorable struggle for the preservation of their personal and political rights.

Mr. CLARK, of Missouri. I hope the gentleman will permit me to make a suggestion. Did the people of Kansas confine their resistance entirely to Territorial laws?

Mr. PARROTT. They did; but I am now on the point of the Territorial laws. Mr. Speaker, I recognise nothing as law, except the will of the people legally expressed; and the laws resisted by my constituency—or evaded, is the better term, though I do not shrink from anything in this respect; I say they were spurious and null—the laws they evaded, sir, were not the will of the people legally expressed. No, sir, they were the enactments of a Missouri mob, clothed with the thin semblance of law. They were made in fraud. They were themselves fraud. They were intended to promote and encourage fraud. By means of these pretended enactments, the most refined cruelty was practiced, through the connivance of the District Court—a creation of the usurpation—under whose process grand juries were packed and indictments fabricated against innocent men. The Government never had the hardihood to bring these cases before a traverse jury. And, sir, they were only executed by the aid of Federal appointees, sent to that Territory from abroad. The largest bounties of Federal patronage stimulated these competing scoundrels to outdo each other in works of infamous rascality. [Sensation and laughter.] They never found, and they never could find, citizens of Kansas Territory who would stand up in favor of these pretended laws.

Sir, when you come to speak of devotion to law, I challenge any man to show me a constituency which has sacrificed more in behalf of the institutions and laws of the country than that which I am proud to represent and defend upon this floor. They have submitted even to the color of Federal authority, in my judgment, not always wisely; but they have done so. They have had their peaceable political conventions broken up by United States soldiery. They have had their homes desolated and laid waste, and their lives imperilled, by commissioned mobs, sailing through the country for the purpose of hunting out and hounding down every man who resisted their cruel exactions. The whole land has been filled with the fury and passions of Pandemonium by the exercise of pretended Federal authority in that Territory. They have always submitted to these exactions, however unjust.

I know that it is indeed difficult for men to maintain such a position; and I am not at all surprised, Mr. Speaker, that partisan zeal should have heaped upon my constituency the charge of revolutionary conduct. It is indeed difficult to draw the line between legitimate and illegitimate opposition. They have chosen, sir, to submit, and to take the consequences, as a lesser evil than the odium of insurrection. There may have been—there has been—an occasional exceptional adventurer, who, in the fury of passion, raised his arm against the authority of the United States; but that has been a bubble upon the surface—a pimple on the skin—the great popular heart has been sweet and sound to the core in loyalty and devotion to the institutions of the country. So much for that.

I come now, Mr. Speaker, to consider further the objections which are stated in the minority report. It is said that there are not enough people in the Territory; and that, sir, is said by the gentleman from Missouri, [Mr. CLARK,] in the face of the fact, that, with little more than one-half the present population, he proffered a willing and long-continued support to the Lecompton Constitution. But these objectors are of two classes: the first, who deny that there is sufficient population in the Territory; and the second, who, if there be sufficient population, deny that that sufficiency has been legally ascertained. I reply to the first class by saying it is not true in point of fact that there are not ninety-three thousand people in the Territory of Kansas. I have four distinct sources from which I derive my information upon that subject. The first is, the actual vote polled at the general elections of 1859; the second, registered voters of the Territory; the third, a census taken by the people; and the fourth, the taxable property assessed by the assessors of the Territory. They all agree in making the aggregate population of the Territory at least ninety-three thousand people.

I will say here, in answer to the interrogatory of the gentleman from New Jersey, [Mr. ADRAIN,] put to me a while ago, that the population of Kansas does not fall short of one hundred thousand, in my judgment. We have, first, over twenty thousand people registered of of six months' residence. We have, in the second place, two general elections—the election on the ratification of the Constitution, and the election for Delegates to Congress—at each of which, 17,000 votes were cast. I ask gentlemen upon all sides, who are familiar with these things, how many voters they suppose, in a scattered Territory like ours, from some inability or another, were kept away from the polls? It is not too much to say, and hardly, I think, too much to ask from a candid opponent, the concession that there must be at least, when seventeen thousand votes have been polled at three general elections, twenty thousand voters in that Territory.

Mr. REAGAN. Let me put a question to the gentleman. I do so for the purpose of eliciting information. Is the number of population stated by the gentleman the number that is included within the boundaries of the proposed new State, as prescribed in the pending bill; or are the people outside of the western boundary of the proposed new State included in his statement? Does he embrace the Pike's Peak settlers?

Mr. PARROTT. I am going to consider the census, about which something has already been said; and I may say, in reference to the interrogatory of the gentleman from Texas, [Mr. REAGAN,] that the population disclosed by these elections, and by the census which has been taken, is, none of it, included in the region cut off and now known as Pike's Peak.

Mr. REAGAN. Let me understand the gentleman. Does he say that his aggregate embraces none of the people of what is known as the Pike's Peak region.

Mr. PARROTT. I say that the people who live in what is now known as Pike's Peak, and outside of the western boundary of the proposed new State, are not included in any of these estimates.

Mr. BARKSDALE. Has the gentleman in his possession the returns taken under the census? If he has, I would like to have the exact figures.

Mr. PARROTT. I am coming to that. I am reluctant, Mr. Speaker, to put my own testimony in; but it will be remembered by gentlemen, and it has been reproduced here this morning, that the Delegate from Oregon, when similarly situated to myself, offered his testimony, and it was accepted, and I believe acted upon at least by a respectable portion of the opposite side of the House. It is for this reason that I have, in this connection, stated my own conviction of the sufficiency of population. I hold in my hand a report made by a committee—the Committee on Elections of the late Territorial Legislature of Kansas. I call the attention of the gentleman from Mississippi [Mr. BARKSDALE] to it. It is a report on an imperfect and fragmentary census taken in June, 1859, by order of the Legislature, for purposes of *taxation*, having no reference to the requirements of the English bill. *None* of the counties are fully reported, and many made no return at all. What I am now going to read, is a revision of this census by the last Legislature.

Mr. BARKSDALE. I would inquire if that census was taken under an act authorized by the Legislature of Kansas.

Mr. PARROTT. I so stated. Since that time, the immigration into Kansas has been unprecedented. I was saying, that the Committee on Elections in the Legislature of Kansas, to which was referred the subject of the census, reported as follows:

"The Committee on Elections, to whom was 'referred the subject of the census, have had 'the subject under consideration, and ask leave 'to submit the following report:

"Your committee have examined the re'turns as submitted with the Governor's mes'sage, and find from information obtained from 'the clerks of the several counties returned, 'and members who represent those counties in 'both branches of the Legislature, that the re'turns are very imperfect; that in many coun'ties only partial returns have been received by 'the Executive, as required by law.

"Your committee find that Doniphan coun'ty has returned, from four townships, eleven 'hundred and eleven registered votes, and a 'population of thirty-five hundred and nine; 'and, from reliable information before the com'mittee, the registers of that county now show 'a registered vote of over eighteen hundred, 'which would make an additional population 'of about three thousand.

"Atchison returned nine hundred and sixty'three registered votes and a population of 'thirty seven hundred and twenty-three, and 'now has on the register about two thousand 'votes, which would make an additional popu'lation of forty-two hundred.

"Riley county is not returned, in which there 'are now about six hundred and fifty votes, 'with a population of about twenty-six hun'dred.

"Leavenworth county has returned a vote of 'three thousand four hundred and forty-five, 'and a population of twelve thousand one hun'dred and twenty-two. The population at that 'time in the city of Leavenworth was nearly 'the amount returned from the whole county. 'From the most reliable information obtained 'from persons well acquainted and represent'ing that county here, the county contains a 'population of sixteen thousand, making an 'additional population of about four thousand.

"From information from the deputy clerk of 'Lykens county, between three and four hun'dred registered voters do not appear in the re'port, that were registered in that county, which 'would make an additional population of about 'sixteen hundred.

"Morris, Pottawatomie, and Washington 'counties, only partial returns, and in some of 'the counties where there are six hundred 'voters, with a population of twenty-five hun'dred, only fifty to two hundred registered 'votes returned.

"In the five counties above mentioned, there 'is returned a population of seventeen hundred 'and eighteen, and a vote of six hundred and 'sixty-four, in the aggregate being less than 'one-third of the actual vote or population in 'said counties, which, if added to the popula'tion now returned, would swell the population 'to the number of about seven thousand.

'This calculation is based on the information 'of persons living in those counties, who have 'examined the census returns and register. 'The census returns, as exhibited in the report 'of the Governor, show great neglect on the 'part of the assessors in many of the town-'ships, and in many of the most populous 'counties. Besides the five mentioned above, 'only three out of five, or five out of eight of 'the townships, have been returned to the Ex-'ecutive, showing conclusively that a very 'large population exists in those counties, of 'which your committee have not been able to 'collect any information as to the real number.

"Your committee also find no returns from 'the counties of Clay, Dickinson, McGee, 'Osage, Wilson, and Dorn, and the smallest 'estimate that can be made is one hundred 'and fifty votes to each county, making a total 'vote of nine hundred, with a population of at 'least thirty-four hundred. This calculation 'is not based on the rapid increase of popula-'tion which has been continually pouring into 'these fertile counties for the last eight months.

"The returns, as reported by the Governor, 'show a partial and incorrect census, as taken 'in the month of June, 1859, since which time 'the emigration into Kansas has been unpre-'cedented. The whole amount of population, 'as reported by the Governor at the regular 'session, was seventy-one thousand seven hun-'dred and seventy; to which, if we add the 'calculation as estimated in the foregoing 'counties partially returned, and from which 'we have no return, the population, up to the '1st day of July, 1859, would amount to about 'ninety-seven thousand five hundred and 'seventy, in which is not included a large 'number of the most populous counties, from 'which there have been only a part of the 'townships returned to the Executive. Your 'committee are of the opinion that it will be 'very difficult to obtain any correct census of 'many of those counties upon the frontier of 'the Territory, where the officers do not either 'qualify at all, and enter upon the discharge 'of their duties, or manifest such gross indif-'ference and stupidity as not to make a return 'in any way to comply with the law, either in 'taking or returning the census. Many of the 'counties have not been organized, and there-'fore have no officers, notwithstanding they 'have a large population, of which your com-'mittee have not been able to collect any cor-'rect data.

"Your committee are of the opinion that the 'rapid increase of wealth and population in 'this Territory, and the manifest desire of all 'classes of our prosperous and energetic citi-'zens, demand that some legislation be had, 'relative to the taking of the future census, 'and other valuable statistics of this Territory.

"Your committee have, with some care and 'labor, prepared a bill and tabular form, which 'they believe will meet the demands of the 'case at this time, and ask leave to submit the 'same with this report, and recommend its 'passage.

"P. P. ELDER, *Chairman.*
"F. M. CHRISTISON.
"J. C. LAMBDIN."

Mr. JOHN COCHRANE. What committee reported that?

Mr. PARROTT. The Committee on Elections of the Legislature of Kansas, and it is signed by Messrs. Elder, Lambdin, and Christison; the last named is a Democrat.

For the purpose of testing the accuracy of that calculation, allow me to call the attention of those who are listening to this part of my argument, to a comparison of what the committee reported, and some returns which I myself have taken the pains to procure. For example, they say:

"Your committee find that Doniphan county 'has returned from four townships eleven hun-'dred and eleven registered votes, and a popu-'lation of thirty-five hundred and nine; and, 'from reliable information before the commit-'tee, the registers of that county now show a 'registered vote of over eighteen hundred, which 'would make an additional population of about 'three thousand."

I hold in my hand the returns from the county clerk of Doniphan county, sworn to and certified by a notary public, in which the aggregate population of that county, as returned to him officially, is put at seven thousand nine hundred and sixty-three, making, as you will see by comparing it with the statements of the committee, a large excess in favor of the official and reliable statement procured from the clerk, under oath.

The same thing is true in regard to Atchison county. There are at least one thousand more people in that county than are reported by this Committee on Elections. There are three thousand more people in my own county—the county of Leavenworth—than are allowed in that report. Taking these statements all together, and this census, as it is completed in this report—which is a *quasi*-official census, because the supplementary returns are completed by the Legislature, or under their sanction—we find a population of over ninety-seven thousand people. I do not doubt, in reality, that it is one hundred thousand.

Mr. BARKSDALE. The gentleman says this census was ordered by the people. I desire to know if the gentleman means that the Territorial Legislature ordered it?

Mr. PARROTT. That is what I mean. So much, then, for the census; so much for the registered vote, and so much for the votes actually polled in three general elections in the Territory. Now, when Oregon was before the House for admission, Mr. Stephens, of Georgia, then the leader of that side of the House, and particularly upon that question, placed great emphasis upon the fact that the taxable property of Oregon furnished sufficient data upon which to compute the population of that Territory. And I say now that the $15,000,000 property listed by the assessors, and reported to the Legislature by the auditor of the Territory, would give that Territory over one hundred and fifty thousand population, if computed upon the basis of the State of Ohio, for example.

I do not claim infallibility for any such test, because I remember that Mr. Stephens got about two hundred and fifty thousand people in Oregon by that calculation, while nobody believes that fifty thousand were there. But as that has been made one of the bases of calculation in ascertaining the population of a Territory, it is no more than just and fair that it should be submitted to the House upon this occasion. Now, one word to the other class of objectors, to wit: those who stick for a legal census by the Federal authorities. Why did you not take the census according to the law? Not only have you failed to do so; but more, you expressly declined to do so, by defeating an appropriation last year in the Senate which you had the power to carry. It seems to me you stultify yourselves; "no one can take advantage of his own wrong." This is a waiver of the point. Otherwise you might make our exclusion perpetual, or at least dependent on your will, by refusing to take a census from time to time. We show the population; to count them was your business, not ours. Moreover, I desire to observe in this place, as conclusive of the "animus" of the Administration or Lecompton party, that the United States marshal of Kansas applied last summer to the Secretary of the Interior for permission to take the census, proposing to wait for his pay till Congress should make an appropriation for that purpose. The offer was declined; much, I think, to the advantage of the marshal.

Now, Mr. Speaker, allow me to say a word in regard to another ground of objection, and that is in respect to the Indians, which so trouble the gentleman from Missouri, [Mr. Clark.] It seems to me to be a sufficient and complete answer to all that has been said in respect to these Indian reservations, that if the rights of the Indians do rest upon a treaty stipulation, then the State Constitution, as to that treaty, is inoperative and void. A treaty stipulation is well known to be a higher law than a State Constitution, and hence, *pro tanto*, to the extent that they conflict, the treaty stipulation will bear down the State Constitution, and this reserve will stand. It appears to be the object of the gentleman from Missouri and his party, having failed to crush out the white man in Kansas by thrusting the black bondman upon him, now to strike another blow by putting the red man in the path of his future progress. This new-born sympathy comes from a suspicious quarter, and at a suspicious time, and I must be allowed to say that I believe it to be manufactured for the occasion. What are the facts? The facts are, that the Cherokee nation always repudiated the possession of this strip of neutral land. I spoke the other day with the chief of that semi civilized nation, and he said that the treaty of 1835 was known among his people as "*the squaw treaty;*" that it was brought about by the imbecility or intoxication of the head men of the nation; that this strip of land was imposed upon them in lieu of $500,000, which the Government had stipulated and agreed to pay. Now they are here, and for what purpose? To complain that we have extended our boundaries over the neutral land, and to complain of a violation of treaty stipulation? Not at all. They are here to complain that the Government will insist upon their having that piece of land, which they did not want and never did own. They are soliciting the President to open negotiations, looking to a retrocession of this tract. I have no doubt that this will, ere long, be brought about.

Mr. HINDMAN. As the gentleman has referred to the attitude held by the Cherokee delegation here, I can speak, from personal knowledge, as to the position they occupy in regard to that neutral land. They do protest against including that territory within the limits of any organized State or Territory.

Mr. STEVENS, of Pennsylvania. Allow me one question. Did the Indians take possession, and are they now inhabiting this land?

Mr. PARROTT. I was going to observe further, Mr. Speaker, in respect to the facts of this case, that, instead of the Indians having asserted any ownership or inhabitancy in that tract known as the "neutral land," there are to-day at least seven hundred white families living on that reservation.

Mr. HINDMAN. Will the gentleman allow me to state, further, that these parties are there in violation of the rights of the Cherokee nation; and that they have been notified by the Commissioner of Indian Affairs that they must remove from the land which they are occupying unlawfully?

Mr. PARROTT. That is another question. The gentleman from Arkansas has not heard of their going off; and he will not, in my opinion.

Mr. MAYNARD. I ask whether this boundary does not include other Indian lands besides these neutral lands?

Mr. PARROTT. No, sir.

Mr. MAYNARD. I am informed very differently.

Mr. PARROTT. It does not. And, moreover, the setting off this tract of land to the Cherokees was itself a violation of this treaty, (I hope the gentleman from Missouri will pay attention to what I am saying,) which provided that the territory to be given to the Cherokees should be a *compact* territory; whereas there is another piece of territory extending between the Cherokee neutral lands and the great body of their possession—I mean the Qua-pau reservation.

Mr. PHELPS. The tract of eight hundred thousand acres of land, to which the gentleman from Kansas refers, is known on the border as the neutral land. It was set apart, and specifically designated as a tract of land containing eight hundred thousand acres. It is, to a certain extent, detached; and yet it is connected on the west with the Cherokee lands.

Mr. PARROTT. Well, I do not care to be further interrupted on this point. I will give the law and the facts bearing on the point at issue.

Mr. PHELPS. That country is embraced within the treaty of 1835; and there is an express stipulation that, of the lands thus assigned to the Cherokee nation, none shall be embraced within the limits of any State, or any organized Territory.

Mr. PARROTT. Well, you did not think of that, I suppose, when you voted for Lecompton. If any gentleman wants to answer the observation which I make on this subject, and which I think complete, I will yield the floor to him to do so; that is, that if there is a treaty stipulation which preserves this land from being surrounded by State or Territorial lands, the State Constitution is, to that extent, inoperative upon it; and with that suggestion, which I think exhaustive, I leave the matter.

Mr. HINDMAN. Is not the gentleman from Kansas aware of the fact, that many years ago the Cherokee country in Georgia was included within the limits of that State; and that a question arose between the State authorities and the Cherokees, and that, in the end, the Cherokees were compelled to emigrate west of the Mississippi river? Just precisely such another controversy will arise in Kansas, if she be admitted under the Wyandotte Constitution.

Mr. PARROTT. Who expects, Mr. Speaker, to stop the progress of white people, or to stop the admission of any State, by the obstacle of an Indian reservation? Our "manifest destiny" is to cover the continent now lying waste with free States. The black race and the red race are fated to fade and be scattered before the advancing whites, "like leaves before the autumn blast." I leave this part of the subject, again repeating, however, that this objection does not lie in the mouths of those who supported the Lecompton Constitution with a similar provision.

I have answered, Mr. Speaker, as I think fairly and candidly, the objections raised by my friend from Missouri. I have shown, I believe, that there is a sufficient population in the Territory. I have shown that the people have adopted a Constitution which no one here will question is the embodiment of their will. It is a fact on which I congratulate myself and the country, that, after all the turbulent and revolutionary proceedings that have taken place in this House and elsewhere in regard to Constitutions, we come here at last with a Constition on which there is no imputation of fraud, and no question that it is the choice of the people. They have, on three, four, or five distinct occasions—each time, as it seems to me, rising to a higher pitch of enthusiasm and excitement, declared in favor of the Wyandotte Constitution as their organic law. Now, I ask, is it fair, is it just and manly, on the part of our Democratic adversaries, to continue to annoy and vex those against whom they have expended all the artillery of legitimate warfare, by attempting to prolong the controversy, by pleading in our ears these hollow-sounding, tinkling technicalities? Would it not be more decorous for them to submit to the inevitable chances of the war which they themselves invoked? It will not be pretended that on the fields of Kansas they have not had a fair opportunity to try the virtues of Southern courage and Southern emigration. If we of the North have surpassed them in our mobility, and maintained the field against their arms, let them yield to the consequences. But I do insist on it, that it does not seem to me to be manly "to stick in the bark," and plead technicalities against those who have, in honorable warfare, overcome them. I would suggest to these gentlemen, that to defeat may be sometimes added dishonor, and to weakness contempt.

There is another consideration connected with the admission of this State, which I ought, in all justice, to submit to the House; and that arises out of the inability of the Territorial Government to afford protection to the property and persons and the political privileges of the people. These Territorial Governments, Mr. Speaker, are, in their best estate, only tolerable, because they are supposed to be unavoidable. I do not mean now to enter that field of dialectics and speculation, whither so many have been lured by cross-purposes, in quest of facts to sustain preconceived opinions. Among the throng of amateurs and experts who hasten to theorize and declaim on mooted points of Territorial government, it may not be unwise to listen for a moment to one who speaks not of theories, but actualities; not of fancies, but of facts; "all of which he saw, and part of which he was."

Now I say, in respect to this Government, following the popular nomenclature of the day, that it is neither "Congressional sovereignty" nor "popular sovereignty." It is a kind of hybrid, and I should style it a *Presidential* or *Executive sovereignty*. In other words, I assert that the Executive influence of the country has pervaded and colored the politics of the Territory under this organic act. I know that much is to be attributed to the grossest vices of maladministration in the Territory; but, after all, taking the plain, legal provisions of the law, which gives the whole judiciary, the whole executive, and two-thirds of the legislative power into the hands of Federal appointees, who go out like prætors in the provinces to rob and squeeze the people whom they are sent to foster and protect—men who are responsible, not to the people, but to their masters at Washington—I say that, giving this power into their hands, you will not find that the popular element can resist its aggressions. It is idle to tell those whose necks are galled and raw, chafing with the yoke of despotism, that they are living in the enjoyment of popular sovereignty. It is idle to tell those who have been robbed of two Legislatures, who have lost three years representation on this floor, who have been wasted by unprovoked wars, who have been stripped of millions worth of private property, that they are in the exercise of any great and desirable species of sovereignty. Wherever the purpose of the Government of the United States and the popular will of Kansas have come in collision, the people have uniformly been borne down. Have they not a housand times, and in a thousand ways, declared that they were unfriendly to the institu-ion of slavery? And has not the Government easserted and persisted in declaring that sla-ery exists there? And does it not keep it here now, to-day, an empty husk?

If, then, the majority have been controlled y the minority; or, in other words, if the peo-le have been borne down by the Government arty; if the policy of the Territory has run ounter to public opinion—that is to say, has een imposed by foreign aid—is it not a palpa-le and ridiculous misnomer, a plain perversion f terms, to call such a scheme a popular Government? To characterize the Territorial Government of which I am speaking, in plain erms, by the lights of experience, I should call a system of Federal police, expanding or ontracting its powers to suit the emergency of he time, and enforcing its arbitrary regula-ions by just so much and such kind of coercion s the occasion may demand. It has been eighed in the balance, and found wanting in verything which tends to preserve the peace nd order of society.

I will say, therefore, of this middle species of overeignty, so-called *popular*, that because it infected with the virus of Executive influence nd dictation, because it is the imposing shib-oleth of party demagogues, and not the choice the well-wishers of the people, it ought to be ondemned and forever discarded. Let us have e thing or the other. Let us have the gov-nment of Congress, or a government of the ople—and by that, I mean the people elect-g all their officers in the Territory; and let ose officers be the servants and not the mas-rs of the people, and respond directly for their nduct to the people. We have tried the esent plan, and we give our testimony against

Our experience reminds me, Mr. Speaker, nothing so much as of the barren honor ich Sancho Panza enjoyed in the govern-nt of his island, which he was glad, with an empty stomach, to abdicate and return to the grateful obscurity from which he had emerged. We would as gladly give up the empty pageant of power for a substantial and just Government, either exerted by Congress or given to the people themselves. For myself, I am satisfied and convinced that the people of the Territory are the just depositary of political power; that they ought to exercise it; and that a Government thus established and power thus exercised will comport with every beneficial end for which Governments are instituted. We have now demonstrated the superior mobility of the Northern people, and their superior energy; and, I expect, in avowing my fidelity to this policy, that nothing but free States will be made all over the unsettled area of the West.

There is another consideration, Mr. Speaker, to which I desire to allude very briefly. There are new Territories arising and pressing upon the borders of Kansas, and it is time that Kansas should be taken out of the way of these new Territories. Four or five Delegates are now waiting at your door to obtain recognition; and it is not too much to say that the next half century will show a numerical majority of States west of the Mississippi river, a large part of which now lie within the unsettled area stretching from the falls of the Missouri to the mouth of the Gila—a region we now know of unsurpassed richness in every element of physical strength. There is the Pike's Peak country—the young Ophir of the West—Jefferson, already grown too large for the swaddling-bands and leading-strings of Territorial government. It needs nothing to hasten its incubation. It will be here thundering at your door as a State next year, and Kansas must be removed to make way for this and other coming States.

There is another consideration, Mr. Speaker, which I must not omit to mention. The commerce of the plains is now beginning, deservedly, to attract the attention of commercial men in every part of the world. That commerce, although yet in its infancy, rivals the commerce of the sea and the commerce of our Western rivers. It needs protection against the bands of nomadic savages which sweep over and infest those Western plains, securing a scanty and precarious subsistence by plunder and the chase. How will you protect it? You must do it by building up an interoceanic railway; and you must do it, further, by pushing forward the breast-work of States, by fortifying the country with stable Governments, and opening its wastes to the careful and productive hands of industry. The commerce which will soon be passing over that country will more than justify the legislation which I ask. You have your gold, and silver, and quicksilver, from Pike's Peak; your wool and hides from New Mexico; your precious ores from Nevada. You will soon have spices, and silks, and teas, from the East, pouring along that great railway; and to prepare the way, to lay the foundation, to do your part towards the realization of this vast enterprise, I ask you to begin, as an important step, in my judgment, with the admission of Kansas into the Union.

Mr. Speaker, I have submitted in this desultory way the considerations which occurred to my mind in regard to this controversy, and I have replied as well as I may to the arguments which have been adduced against the admission of Kansas. I do not propose to indulge in any discussion of the merely political aspect of this question. I may do so at another time. But I will say this: if gentlemen cannot answer these facts and arguments, may I not reasonably anticipate that they will not deny and refuse the conclusions to which they lead?

I indulge, then, the pleasing anticipation that the State will be admitted, and the controversy so far closed. Though the Lecompton Constitution is dead, its offspring, the English bill, still languishes on the statute book—a monument of the folly, the incapacity, and the pernicious politics, of the present Administration. Sponge out this obsolete and inoperative enactment. May I not venture to remind you that those who now plead for justice at your hands are brothers of your blood—revering the same Constitution, obeying the same laws, speaking the same language, cherishing the same traditions of the past, elevated and inspired by the same hopes of future greatness for our country? They have trod the "winepress" of persecution with unflagging firmness, and come forth with a spirit worn, it may be, but unbroken; jubilant, and even defiant; ready to do battle in behalf of truth, justice, humanity, and all things else which contribute to dignify and ennoble a people in the judgment of an enlightened world. With the consummation of this measure we shall, I trust, see an era of better feeling initiated. The distempers generated by this long and fierce controversy will be like volcanoes burnt out—on the ashes, lava, and squalid scoriæ of which shall spring "the peaceful olive and the cheering vine."

PRESIDENTIAL CAMPAIGN OF 1860.

REPUBLICAN EXECUTIVE CONGRESSIONAL COMMITTEE.

HON. PRESTON KING, N. Y., *Chairman.*
" J. W. GRIMES, IOWA.
" L. F. S. FOSTER, CONN.
On the part of the Senate.

HON. JOHN COVODE, PENN., *Treasurer.*
" E. G. SPAULDING, N. Y.
" J. B. ALLEY, MASS.
" DAVID KILGORE, INDIANA.
" J. L. N. STRATTON, N. J.
" E. B. WASHBURNE, ILLINOIS.
On the part of the House of Reps.

The Committee are prepared to furnish the following Speeches and Documents:

EIGHT PAGES.

Hon. W. H. Seward: State of the Country.
" W. H. Seward: "Irrepressible Conflict" Speech.
" G. A. Grow, Penn.: Free Homes for Free Men.
" James Harlan, Iowa: Shall the Territories be Africanized?
" John Hickman, Penn.: Who have Violated Compromises.
" B. F. Wade, Ohio: Invasion of Harper's Ferry.
" G. W. Scranton and J. H. Campbell, Penn.: The Speakership.
" F. P. Blair, Mo., Address at Cincinnati: Colonization and Commerce.
" Orris S. Ferry, Conn.
" Abraham Lincoln, Ill.: The Demands of the South—The Republican Party Vindicated.
" William Windom, Minn.: The Homestead Bill—Its Friends and its Foes.
" Owen Lovejoy, of Illinois: The Barbarism of Slavery.
" Henry L. Dawes, Mass.: The New Dogma of the South—"Slavery a Blessing."
" R. H. Duell, N. Y.: The Position of Parties.
" M. S. Wilkinson, Minn.: The Homestead Bill.
" D. W. Gooch, Mass.: Polygamy in Utah.
Carl Schurz, Wis.: Douglas and Popular Sovereignty.
Lands for the Landless—A Tract.
The Poor Whites of the South—The Injury done them by Slavery—A Tract.

SIXTEEN PAGES.

Hon. Lyman Trumbull, Ill.: Seizure of the Arsenals at Harper's Ferry, Va. and Liberty, Mo., and in Vindication of the Republican Party.
" B. F. Wade, Ohio: Property in the Territories.
" C. H. Van Wyck, N. Y.: True Democracy—History Vindicated.

Hon. H. Wilson, Mass.: Territorial Slave Code.
" John P. Hale, N. H.
" J. J. Perry, Me.: "Posting the Books between the North and the South."
" J. R. Doolittle, Wis.: The Calhoun Revolution—Its Basis and its Progress.
" C. B. Sedgwick, N. Y.: The Republican Party the Result of Southern Aggression.
" M. J. Parrott, Kansas: Admission of Kansas.
Federalism Unmasked: Or the Rights of the States, the Congress, the Executive, and the People, Vindicated against the Encroachments of the Judiciary, prompted by the Modern Apostate Democracy. Being a Compilation from the Writings and Speeches of the Leaders of the Old Jeffersonian Republican Party. By Daniel R. Goodloe.

TWENTY-FOUR PAGES.

Hon. Jacob Collamer, Vermont.

THIRTY-TWO PAGES.

Hon. Thomas Corwin, of Ohio.

GERMAN.

EIGHT PAGES.

Hon. G. A. Grow, Penn.: Free Homes for Free Men.
" James Harlan, Iowa: Shall the Territories be Africanized?
" John Hickman, Penn.: Who Have Violated Compromises.
" William Windom, Minn.: The Homestead Bill—Its Friends and its Foes.
" H. Winter Davis, Md.: Election of Speaker.
Carl Schurz, Wis.: Douglas and Popular Sovereignty.

SIXTEEN PAGES.

Hon. Lyman Trumbull, Ill.: Seizure of the Arsenals at Harper's Ferry, Va., and Liberty, Mo., and in Vindication of the Republican Party.
" W. H. Seward, N. Y.: The State of the Country.
Lands for the Landless—A Tract.

And all the leading Republican Speeches as delivered.

During the Presidential Campaign, Speeches and Documents will be supplied at the following reduced prices: per 100—8 pages 50 cents, 16 pages $1, and larger documents in proportion. Address either of the above Committee.

GEORGE HARRINGTON, *Secretary.*

www.ingramcontent.com/pod-product-compliance
Lightning Source LLC
LaVergne TN
LVHW020638110826
845149LV00004B/1273

* 9 7 8 1 4 1 8 1 8 9 9 5 2 *